We Do It All

Occupation Learning Coloring Book

Volume 1

By Tara Seals

@ 2021 COPYRIGHT All rights reserved. The author retains all copyrights in any text, graphic images, and photos in this book. No part of this publication may be reproduced or transmitted in any form or by any means, electronic or mechanical, including photocopying, recording, or any information storage and retrieval system, without permission in writing from the author.
This book may be published for educational, business, or sale promotional use. For information, please contact the Special Markets Division. Send an email to Info@TheBossyEducator.com with your request.
ISBN: 978-0-578-86955-1
Printed in the United States of America
Published by Able Publishing
Illustrated by Raf Has
Editor: L. B. Cadogan

This book belongs to:

_____

Dedication

This occupation learning coloring book is dedicated to the thousands of students I have taught during my amazing journey. I will always and forever encourage you to live life to the absolute fullest and do it YOUR way. Execution over thinking! Twelve options are presented here, but know your options are limitless. Continue to make yourself proud and always remember, bossy is as bossy does!

Table of Contents

Page	Occupation
1	Private Tutor
2	Restaurant Owner
3	Barber
4	E-Commerce Store Owner
5	Natural Hair Stylist
6	Software Developer
7	Transportation Service Provider
8	Baker
9	Real Estate Developer
10	Manicurist/Pedicurist
11	Event Planner
12	Cosmetologist

Private Tutor

Private Tutor – I privately teach and help children learn how to read, write, compute, comprehend, and grow in all academic areas, usually 1-on-1 or in a small group.

Restaurant Owner

Restaurant Owner – I own, operate, and manage restaurants using my own special recipes and secret ingredients. I hire chefs, managers, hosts/hostesses, custodians, and overall staff for the restaurant.

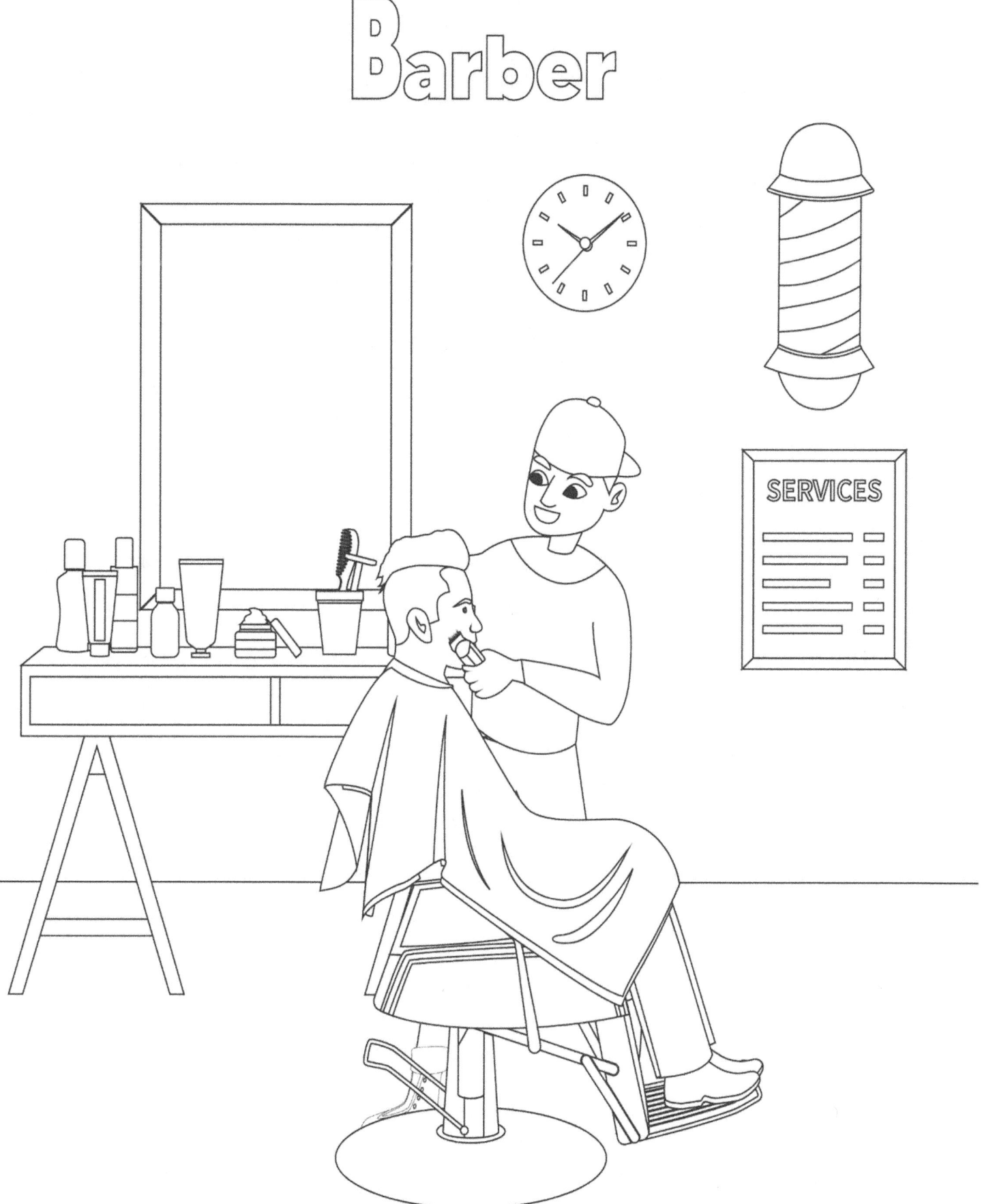

Barber - I provide services such as haircuts, undercuts, and beard services. I help men and women maintain their grooming needs.

E-Commerce Store Owner

E-Commerce Store Owner – I create unique brands and design online stores based on physical or digital products and/or services. I create, sell, fulfill, and ship the final product to the buyer.

Natural Hair Stylist

Natural Hair Stylist – I take care of your natural tresses and afro-textured or kinky hair, and use techniques such as twisting, locking, braiding, etc.

Software Developer - I analyze the needs of target audiences, and design, test, and develop solution-based software to solve problems and meet the needs of users.

Transportation Service Provider

Transportation Service Provider – I transport goods and passengers from one location to another. I partner with local and global companies to provide transportation services.

Baker

Baker – I bake amazing foods using only the best ingredients. From pastries to cakes to pies, every bite will melt in your mouth.

Real Estate Developer

Real Estate Developer – I formulate, create, and orchestrate the process of real estate development from the beginning to the end. I buy land, finance real estate deals or pay cash, and build or have builders build homes or commercial development projects.

Manicurist/Pedicurist

Manicurist/Pedicurist - I clean, file, trim, polish, and repair fingernails and toenails. I also apply artificial nails using specialized techniques and decorate nails and toes with nail art.

Event planner – I coordinate and manage all aspects of events. I scout and select locations, solicit bids, maintain vendor relationships and client communications, negotiate contracts, arrange transportation, and oversee budgets.

Cosmetologist

Tasha's Beauty Parlor & Lounge

OPEN

Welcome

Cosmetologist – I provide cosmetic treatments to the hair, skin, and nails. I shampoo, condition, cut, color, and style natural or chemically-treated hair.

We Do It All Worksheet

1. P _ _ _ _ _ _   U _ R
2. _ S _ _ _ _ T _ _ E _
3. _ A _ _ R
4. _ _ C _ _ _ E _ S _ _ O _ _ _
5. A T _ _ _ _   I _ _ _ _ S
6. S _ T _ _ _ _ V _ _ _ _
7. R _ S _ _ _ _ _ _ _ _ _   _ V _ _ _
   _ _ _ P _ _ _ _
8. _ _ R
9. E _ _ T _ _ _ _ _ O _
10. M _ _ _ _ _ _ _ / _ D U _
11. _ _ N _ _ _ N N _
12. C _ M _ _ _ _ _ T

THE END

NOTES:

www.ingramcontent.com/pod-product-compliance
Lightning Source LLC
Chambersburg PA
CBHW081157290426

44108CB00018B/2587